Dance in the Fullness of Joy!

Ala Carter

SURRENDER TO JOY

Published by Mater Media
St. Louis, Missouri
www.matermedia.org

Cover and Interior Design: Trese Gloriod

Printed in the USA.

ISBN: 978-0-9913542-6-9

SURRENDER TO
JOY

Called to My Knees to Rise with Christ

Allan Barton

MATER
MEDIA

**MATER
MEDIA**

Mater Media is pleased to publish this memoir of a man whose life was redirected by God in an extraordinary way. As a result of his spiritual transformation over a 30-year period, Allan Barton has been the hands and heart of Christ, visiting thousands of the sick and elderly in nursing homes and hospitals. His life is a lesson on how to move from Surrender to Joy.

*"The one who has hope lives differently; the one
who hopes has been granted the gift of a new life."*

Pope Benedict XVI

DEDICATION

To my grandsons, Luke and Jack.

I wonder how old Luke and Jack will be when their father feels that they are ready to read this book. Last year, Luke celebrated his sixth birthday, and Jack, his fifth, while their Papa was looking over his shoulder past 70. I sensed that they were growing up too fast, and it occurred to me that when they are old enough to seriously consider the most important questions in life about who God is, who they are, and what God's plan is for them, I may not be around to share my thoughts on those most important subjects. That possibility motivated me to write this book.

I recently drove Luke home after an overnight stay. I asked him how kindergarten was going. From his car seat in the back, he told me school was fine, and then I asked him what he'd been learning. He mentioned that he was learning about the planets, and he then proceeded to name all the planets in our solar system. Pretty impressive. I asked if he was learning about God and how much God loves him. He answered yes. Then I asked him if he knew that God was bigger than the whole world. He answered, "Papa, God is bigger than the whole universe." I guess I wasn't thinking big enough for Luke.

I hope that Luke and Jack will come to understand that although God is bigger than the whole universe, he is also small enough to live in their hearts.

Jack recently stayed overnight at our house. While we were resting after lunch the next day, he leaned over and asked me, "Papa, will we be pals forever?"

I answered, "Yes, Jack, I will be your pal forever, and Luke's too." I pray that Luke and Jack will always strive to do God's will and come to know that Jesus is their Lord and Savior and that he also wants to be their best pal forever.

Love,
Papa

INTRODUCTION

"Say the secret word and split $100."

Some in my generation might remember that line from the question-and-answer television game show *You Bet Your Life* hosted by comedian Groucho Marx in the 1950s and early '60s. During the interview portion of the program if a contestant said the secret word, a toy duck with eyeglasses and a mustache would drop down with a $100 bill in its beak, and the money would be split by the two contestants.

I believe that God asks each one of us whether we will live according to his will rather than our own. How will we respond to God's call? We need to remember that we are *betting our eternal lives* on our answer. The answer is no secret, but if we are unsure how to answer, we need to first look inside ourselves. God has written the word on the heart of every person. We can look to Jesus, the Incarnate Word of God, who always does the will of his Father. We can look to Mary, the Mother of Jesus, and Saint Joseph, her spouse, who are great exemplars of humility and the obedience of faith. We can also look to the thousands of saints and theologians who have spoken the word for centuries. The word must be "Yes." So simple, yet so difficult to say. When I finally said yes and surrendered to God, it was as if the Holy Spirit descended and gave me the greatest gifts of all—a stronger faith and a deeper relationship with Jesus Christ.

I know I have many times answered God's request either with an emphatic "No" or a flimsy "Maybe." When I finally said a wholehearted "Yes" to God 30 years ago, he began transforming me into the person he desired me to be from the moment he first conceived of me in his mind. If God can do this for me, he can do it for anyone. That is his promise!

My favorite movie scene is the one in *The Passion of the Christ* where Mary comes to Jesus' aid when he falls carrying his cross on the way to his crucifixion and death. She remembers painfully watching him fall while he was running as a child. Now she witnesses his falling again under the weight of the cross. Jesus, in his bloody and weakened condition, looks at her and says, "See, Mother, I make all things new." He is referring to his passion, death, and resurrection that will give mankind a fresh start. He will bear the weight of our sins and give humanity the gift of an abundant life by restoring the intimate relationship between God and mankind that was lost by the sin of Adam and Eve.

I am grateful for his giving me a new life, one that I didn't fully embrace until I decided to live in accordance with God's will, rather than my own.

I am no expert in theology or philosophy. I have no credentials in either discipline. I can only offer witness to certain experiences I have enjoyed over the past 30 years that have strengthened my faith in God and given me a closer personal relationship with Jesus Christ. For many years I have wanted to share my joy by shouting from the rooftops or preaching from the pulpit. Fortunately, common sense has prevailed and I have decided to write this book instead. Besides, I'm too old to be climbing roofs, and I don't want to run off the congregation.

This book is my testimony of how God's grace has blessed me over the past 30 years. It is divided into four parts. *Part I* describes the circumstances leading up to and including my surrender to God's will and reflections on the process that led up to that life-changing moment. *Part II* illustrates how the Holy Spirit began to open my heart and mind to an awakening to God's truth. *Part III* describes certain experiences that led me to the incredible joy found in the realization of God's presence, in receiving and in giving forgiveness, and in sharing the love of God with others. *Part IV* contains reflections on God's universal call to the fullness of life through a total commitment to following his will.

PART I

THE FREEDOM OF SURRENDER

WHO AM I, LORD, THAT YOU ASK FOR MY HEART?

I will give you a new heart and place a new spirit within you, taking from your bodies your stony hearts and giving you natural hearts.

(Ezekiel 36:26)

---- 1 ----

On My Knees

It was the fall of 1989; I was living by myself, having recently separated from my wife of 19 years, my 15-year-old daughter, and my 12-year-old son. My wife and I had spent considerable time in marriage counseling. Unfortunately, the counseling was unsuccessful, and when our relationship became unbearable, I moved out. To make matters even worse, shortly after moving out I was asked to leave the law firm that I joined after graduating from law school 17 years earlier. I was told that I had to leave since my productivity (billable hours) had gone down significantly for a couple of years. I had become obsessed with my marital difficulties and couldn't focus on my work.

In the early months of my separation, I spent a lot of time alone, in reflection. How could this have happened to me? I had been successful in school, in sports, and pretty much everything I tried. I was a partner in a prestigious law firm with a six-figure income, a country club membership, and a large house in an affluent neighborhood. Both of my children attended private schools. I moved in some pretty powerful circles. I had gotten somewhat cocky and probably deserved a piece of humble pie, but the whole pie was hard to digest.

One night I felt so alone, without hope. I had no idea what was coming next. I began to weep heavily. It was one heck of a pity party. (Fortunately, I hadn't invited anyone else to attend.) I went into the bathroom to put a cold washcloth on my face, and when I looked in the mirror, I hardly recognized myself because my face was so red and swollen. I returned to the living room and reflected on how I had always thought I could write the book of my life; everything would go as I planned. I now realized that life didn't work that way.

This new reality was extremely hard to accept. I felt that I had always been in charge of things and now look what a mess I had made of my life. I was a broken man. I sobbed and with a heaving chest, knelt down, surrendered to God, and asked him to take over my life. It had taken me 41 years to say "Yes" to God. I felt a great peace sweep over me.

Putting God in his rightful place as the head of my life freed me from the overwhelming burden of trying to be in charge of everything. It seemed counter-intuitive that I had surrendered, yet now I was free. I had always considered surrender as a negative concept. To surrender was to give up, to lose. You surrendered when you had been beaten by your opponent. If you lost on the battlefield, you surrendered to your enemy. Now I realized that on the spiritual front, surrender meant winning. It must be one of the most profound paradoxes of life that the greatest freedom comes from surrender. I now understood the spiritual necessity of "dying to self."

I had no idea of what would happen next. Rather than immediately planning the next steps for my marriage and my career, I decided to ask God to lead me. The next day I wrote the following prayer, which I tacked to the bulletin board in my kitchen:

Give me an open heart and an open mind
to hear Your message, to keep Your light
burning within me, to see Your light in all others.

Help me make the right choices and decisions
with the wisdom and strength that is Your Divinity.
Help me endure the inevitable pain and suffering
that is my humanity.

Although I had prayed often since I was a child, this was the first prayer that I had written. Usually when I prayed, I asked for something I wanted, such as a good grade on a test. When the prayers were answered, I took all the credit and seldom thanked God for his help. When they weren't answered, sometimes I figured that God didn't care enough about me. I often didn't accept that maybe it wasn't his plan for me to have what I wanted, or that I didn't get the desired result because I failed to do my part. This prayer was different. I believe that the Holy Spirit helped me write it since he knew that it was what God the Father wanted for me. Writing the prayer burned it into my memory. I have recited it often in the past 30 years. God continues to answer my prayer in the most extraordinary ways.

This was the most painful period in my life, yet it was the beginning of a new life healed by the love of God. Through his grace I have been blessed with faith in getting to know Jesus Christ as my Lord, my Savior, my brother, and my friend; with hope in knowing I can place my total trust in Jesus no matter what happens; and with the joy in knowing and sharing the love of God. He has been with me to share my difficult times, including my divorce and annulment, the loss of two more jobs as the result of corporate acquisitions, and the death of my parents and several friends. He has also been with me to share my joys, including my marriage to my current wife, Cyndi; watching my children grow into adult-hood; the birth of my two grandsons; and following my retirement, the privilege of helping to care for my grandsons several days a week during the first few years of their lives.

---| 2 |---

I Will Give You a New Heart

The dreams described in this chapter were at the heart of a short story titled, "A New Day is Dawning," that I wrote after returning from a three-day silent retreat several years ago. On the retreat I had spent several hours reflecting on my life. The dreams are symbolic of the stages that I perceived I had gone through leading up to my surrender to God in October 1989

Dream One. As the dream began, I entered Room 101 of the cardiac surgery wing of a hospital. Standing in front of me was a surgeon who had scrubbed, gowned, and gloved for surgery. He confirmed that all of the tests had been completed and informed me that I was suffering from end-stage advanced heart failure. He told me that unless I received a heart transplant, I would die. He read the results of several diagnostic tests, including blood tests, electrocardiogram, echocardiogram, and an MRI. He asked if I needed any more proof. I told him that he was mistaken, that he must have read someone else's chart. I felt perfectly healthy and certainly didn't need heart surgery.

Reflection. The cardiac surgeon was Jesus, the Divine Surgeon, who had been calling me for many years to a conversion of heart. In Room 101, Jesus told me all the ways I had chosen my will over God's will and that I was now at the point where unless I repented of my sins and acknowledged that God was the ruler of my life, I was in danger of spiritual death. I needed to surrender, seek forgiveness, and ask God for a new spiritual heart. However, I didn't accept Jesus' advice; I thought that he was misjudging me.

Dream Two. I entered Room 102 and faced the same surgeon. He again read from his laptop and strongly recommended that I undergo a heart transplant. I told him I thought that I was pretty healthy and didn't need a heart transplant, but I would consider making a few minor changes to my daily routine by eating less junk food and getting more exercise.

Reflection. After Jesus' admonition, I agreed to make a few minor concessions. I resumed going to Mass on Sundays and tried to follow some of the Church's other rules, but only when it was convenient. I thought this was an adequate response to Jesus' call to conversion. Unfortunately, it didn't make much difference in the way I acted outside of church. I might have been more aware of God's will, but I kept my will on an equal or superior level. If I became aware of a conflict between God's will and my own, I would often rationalize that I could interpret God's will in a way that made it conform to mine. I stayed in Room 102 for many years.

Dream Three. The third dream in Room 103 started as the others, but this time I carefully examined the evidence. It was clear; I accepted the surgeon's diagnosis. However, I wasn't willing to receive a heart transplant. I was too afraid. What if I died on the operating table? At least if I didn't have the surgery, I would still be alive, although maybe for only a short time. Besides, I wondered what it would feel like to have someone else's heart beating in my chest.

Reflection. I'm not sure when in my life I entered Room 103. At some point I became aware that there was something seriously wrong with the direction of my life. In hindsight, I realized that for many years I acted as if only my will determined what was right and wrong. Even though I was aware of God's commandments, I acted without giving them any consideration.

I was doing my will instead of God's, and my life was not going the way I wanted. I was often depressed about my job and my marriage. I needed to make a dramatic change. When Jesus advised me to surrender to God's will and have a spiritual heart transplant, I knew he was right. Unfortunately, for many years I was unwilling to let go of my ego and place my trust in his hands. I was afraid of the unknown. What kind of person would I be? At least I knew myself as I had always been; I didn't have a desire to change. It was fun doing whatever I wanted. Would life be boring if I conformed my life to God's will?

Dream Four. In the final dream the surgeon was waiting for me as I entered Room 104. After repeating his previous warning, he again asked me if I wanted to have the heart transplant. This time I agreed to have the operation and placed my complete trust in his hands. The surgery saved my life. Following the surgery, I was told that in order to keep my new heart in proper condition, I needed to remain vigilant in leading a healthy life style. I was cautioned that I would risk rejecting the new heart if I didn't take the prescribed medication the rest of my life.

Reflection. I entered Room 104 on that night in October 1989 and dropped to my knees. I was ready to respond to the call of Jesus to surrender. I had reached the lowest point in my life as a result of putting myself in charge. I couldn't do it anymore;

I needed to be rescued from the pit. I tearfully responded to Jesus, "Lord, I surrender; I place my total trust in your hands. Yes! Give me a new heart." Jesus looked at me with eyes filled with peace and joy and spoke very gently,

> Allan, we have been calling you to this room long, long, before you were born, hoping that you would choose life. I will give you a new heart. I gave my blood for your transfusion two thousand years ago.

"Lord, how can I repay you?" I asked.

Jesus answered,

> Kneel and give thanks to my Father the Almighty.
> Place your trust under the shadow of the wings
> of the Holy Spirit.
> As for me, Allan, love others as I have loved you,
> and in doing so:
>
> See with my eyes.
> Speak with my voice.
> Touch with my hands.
> Think with my mind.
> Love with My Heart!

I realized that I must commit to living a healthy spiritual life to avoid suffering rejection of my new heart. I must continue to surrender frequently to God's will, or I may find myself roaming the halls of the hospital in the dark, opening the doors to Room

101, 102, or 103. If that happens, I need to pray for Jesus to light the way to Room 104 again.

Several years after writing about the dreams, I attended a retreat with 50 men from my parish. It was a wonderful faith-filled weekend. One of the main themes was answering the call to serving others. When I returned home and unpacked, I noticed the tag on my suitcase with my room number at the retreat center.

It was Room 105.

I interpreted this holy coincidence as a reminder not to remain in Room 104, keeping my new heart to myself, but to enter the world in Room 105, sharing the loving heart of Christ with everyone I encountered.

PART II

THE SURPRISE OF AWAKENING

| WHO AM I, LORD, THAT YOU ASK FOR MY MIND? |

Do not conform yourself to this age, but be transformed by the renewal of your mind, that you may discern what is the will of God, what is good and pleasing and perfect.

(Romans 12:2)

3

Open the Flood Gates

Why was I unwilling or unable to see or hear God's truth before surrendering to his will? After surrendering, I was surprised by the powerful awakening that occurred as God opened my heart and my mind.

How could I have been such a blockhead for so long? Sometimes I think that from an early age—in terms of spiritual matters—my heart and my head were frozen in impenetrable blocks of ice. I had been baptized and confirmed in the Catholic Church, attended Catholic schools through high school, and attended Mass weekly from age 6 until I was 18. Unfortunately, I failed to take the lessons seriously and lived my life as if they had no relevance.

My religion classes through high school in the late 1960s were uninspiring. They were pretty much like any of my other courses, just information to memorize and repeat on tests. My classes in history, physics, French, and most other courses were more appealing than my religion classes. I don't remember much discussion about Jesus or about having a relationship with him. We learned about the sacraments, numerous rules, and a long list of dos and don'ts, which made me feel guilty for not measuring up. There wasn't much emphasis on God's great love, mercy, and forgiveness.

I seldom went to church in college, nor did I take any theology classes. I had become totally indifferent to spiritual matters. I started attending church again on a regular basis when my daughter started kindergarten. Even then, very few of the homilies or scripture readings at church had any effect on my thinking or actions. I wasn't reading any spiritual materials, nor was I participating in any Bible studies or faith discussion groups. I didn't have a regular prayer life. In other words, I was just barely going through the motions. I didn't feel a need to depend on God, since I thought I was doing a pretty good job of taking care of things myself.

When I said yes to God, I was surprised when the warmth of God's grace melted the ice blocks that surrounded my heart and head; the waters flooded my heart with faith and a passionate desire to know God and flooded my head with understanding. The stronger my faith became, the more I wanted to learn; the more I learned, the stronger my faith became. As my faith strengthened, I felt a compelling desire to learn who God is, who I am, and God's plan for me. I asked God to turn me inside out so that I could see my guts, to see myself as he did. God's answer wasn't pleasant to hear. If there were a Sinner's Hall of Shame, I felt that I would have been inducted on the first ballot. Unfortunately, I still maintain my eligibility.

As the list went on, I began to accept responsibility for my part in the failure of my marriage and to understand why my wife ultimately gave up on me. For 19 years she witnessed many times the complete list of my transgressions. I prayed vigorously for the grace to change. I believe the Holy Spirit inspired me to ask for the "strength to be gentle." I realized that strength and gentleness could be compatible. It took more strength for me to be gentle than to demonstrate strength in the negative ways I had learned growing up. I am grateful that God answered my prayer, and I am sure the other people in my life are grateful as well.

There's an expression, "When the student is ready, the teacher (or master) will appear." Before my conversion my stubbornness had locked the classroom door on the inside, keeping Jesus, the teacher, from entering. As a result of my conversion, grace unlocked the door and God began to enlighten my mind, and his truth went straight from my mind to my heart for safekeeping. At other times, it felt as if God were speaking directly to my heart. In response to what I believe were promptings from the Holy Spirit, I started reading one or two spiritual books a week; I couldn't get enough. I often went to daily Mass on my lunch break. I participated in Bible studies and faith-sharing groups. The "Good News" of the Gospel became the "Great News" of my life.

It became a priority to find time each day to enter what author Matthew Kelly calls the "Classroom of Silence," where I could talk to God without any distractions and listen for his response. Unfortunately, often it was very difficult to find any quiet time on those days when I started on full throttle and raced until evening without a pit stop.

One of the greatest gifts I have received has been the opportunity to put my job and all activities aside and give three days to God on a silent retreat. It takes planning and the support of others to set those days aside, but it doesn't seem that great a burden when one considers it constitutes less than one percent of the total year. For the past 28 years, I have attended a three-day silent retreat annually. On every retreat I feel that God is calling me closer to his heart and giving me a three-day personal seminar on sharing his great love and mercy with others. (See Appendix for the poem titled, "Behold the Heart of Jesus," that I wrote on a retreat several years ago.)

4

Seeing the Forest and the Trees

When did I "lose sight of the forest for the trees"? When I was a child, I learned in religion class that my purpose in life was to know, love, and serve God in this life, so that I can be happy with him in heaven (the *Baltimore Catechism*). This was the big picture, the "forest." It was a simple, comforting concept, which at the time was desirable and seemed to be achievable. As I grew older, and life got more complicated, I turned my focus to the ever increasing number of distractions, the "trees" in my life, and lost sight of the forest somewhere along the way.

There were numerous trees in my life that blocked my focus on God, such as school, family, friends, jobs, and the myriad of other ordinary daily experiences of a busy life. There were also several trees darkened by my sinful desires. Two very large trees grew in the middle of my forest that were the greatest obstacles to my vision. The largest tree was the tree of my self-centeredness, my desire to live according to my own rules. With the help of grace, I began to chop down that tree by surrendering to God's will. I was very surprised to discover the identity of the other large tree. It was the Church.

It wasn't the Church per se; it was how I viewed the Church. I only looked at the surface of the Church, including the buildings, the required attendance at Mass, and the myriad of other rules. I didn't go any deeper, and as a result, my experience of God was dry and unfulfilling. I had missed the vision of enjoying a loving relationship with Jesus and sharing with others the love that emanated from our relationship.

After my conversion, I stepped back and took another look at the Church. It was the tallest tree, having grown to its majestic height since being planted by Jesus 2,000 years ago. I noticed that the bark had been scarred by thousands of axe blows inflicted over the centuries, some swung by the arborists whose vocation was to protect and nourish the tree. I was glad that Jesus promised that the Tallest Tree would never perish.

I approached the Tallest Tree, and with a helping hand from the Holy Spirit, I began to climb its sturdy limbs. Upon reaching the top, I emerged above the broad canopy of tree tops. I felt the love of God in the depths of my heart, and once again I saw the purpose of my life, illuminated by the resplendent light of Christ.

Once I rediscovered the forest, I descended the Tallest Tree to the forest floor below and refocused on the other trees, not wanting to "lose sight of the trees for the forest." With God's help I pruned those ordinary trees in my life that had become overgrown from my misplaced priorities. I uprooted the unhealthy trees that had withered from the disease of my sinful habits.

I then studied the Tallest Tree, whose limbs had supported my climb. One of the limbs contained a beautiful altar to worship God and give him praise and thanksgiving. Another limb contained the sacraments instituted by Jesus as sources of grace. There was a long limb embodying the community of believers who constitute the Church, the Body of Christ. There was a limb manifesting the teaching authority of the Church, guiding me in my search for truth. I can't make it on my own. I need the Church; I need to keep it always in my line of sight, not as an obstruction, but as the Tallest Tree that helps lead me to heaven.

God desires that I see both the forest and the trees—to see the truth, beauty, and goodness both in him and in his creation. I need to look at the trees with the fresh eyes of faith, seeing God in the people and the circumstances that fill my days, while at the same time keeping my focus on the purpose of my life.

As I now walk through the thinned-out forest, I listen for God's still, small voice riding the gentle breeze that weaves through the trees, beckoning me to love.

PART III

THE RETURN
OF JOY

WHO AM I, LORD,
THAT YOU ASK ME TO DANCE?

*Restore my joy in your salvation; sustain
in me a willing spirit.*

(Psalm 51:14)

---|5|---

God Within

Music can be a great inspiration for spiritual peace and joy, from the sublime "Panis Angelicus," sung be Andrea Bocelli or Charlotte Church, to the exuberant "I Will Follow Him," sung by Little Peggy March or the nuns and Whoopi Goldberg in the movie *Sister Act*. Sometimes a song or a poem may inspire a listener to hear a spiritual truth in a fresh and exciting way. Shortly after my separation, I was inspired by certain words of a poem by the Irish actor and singer Richard Harris.

Richard Harris performed a dramatic reading of his poem titled, "There Are Too Many Saviors on My Cross," on an album of his greatest hits. I had purchased the album in order to listen to "MacArthur Park." Some people believe it was one of the worst songs of the 1960s. On the other hand, I remembered liking it, because it was so unusual, containing rather bizarre lyrics and playing for over seven minutes.

I didn't expect to receive any spiritual message from "MacArthur Park" or any of the other songs on the album. I was surprised that there was a poem on the album and even more surprised that certain words of the poem sounded like a response to my prayer asking for an open heart and open mind (Chapter 1).

The poem was written as Jesus' response to man's misuse of religion to justify war and other evils, specifically the religious conflict in Northern Ireland. I played it over several times; it was so powerful. Richard Harris's dramatic reading was enhanced by riveting background music. At one point, Jesus' harsh rebuke shifted to a comforting reminder of God's loving presence within each person. It felt like the words were spoken directly to me. I wrote the words down on a scrap of paper and tacked it to the bulletin board in my kitchen below my earlier prayer asking for an open heart and an open mind.

A few days later I noticed that the two pieces seemed to belong together. I then copied them on a separate page with my prayer at the top and what I felt was God's response in the poem at the bottom. I put the name of the author below each part. Under the top part, I wrote "Al." I then considered what name I should attribute to the lower part. While focusing on the words of the poem, it hit me: the name was "I AM."

I felt a chill rush over me, remembering that "I AM" was God's name revealed to Moses from the burning bush. I then titled the prayer "God Within." I stood up and did a celebratory fist pump that would rival one thrust by Tiger Woods after sinking a 40-foot, downhill, double-breaking putt. Wow!

I had heard the comforting message of God's intimate presence dozens of times before, but I had never completely accepted it. I had always thought that it was too good to be true; I was not worthy of such a relationship. Why would God, the powerful creator of the universe, be interested in me, an insignificant creature? Why would God, who is beauty and goodness, want to be so close to an unclean sinner like me? I now understood that God desires a mutually loving relationship with all his children: that is why he created us. Since his love is unconditional, our unworthiness does not diminish God's desire for union with us.

It was surprising how the simple words of a poem had led me to feel the overwhelming joy of God's presence. Was this the Holy Spirit at work again? Since I felt a more intimate relationship with God, our conversations were no longer long- distance calls. I often pray those words of the poem after receiving

Holy Communion and feel a profound sense of Jesus being a part of me.

Finding the poem on the album was an unexpected gift. At that time in my life, I needed reassurance that God was accessible to me and that he would answer my prayers. I now felt confident that I could count on him, and unlike a job or a personal relationship, I could trust that he would never leave me. He would stay with me to guide me in my decisions and support me through life's challenges.

Although I enjoyed listening to "MacArthur Park" again, hearing the comforting words of the poem was the real icing on the cake!

---- 6 ----

The Joy of Forgiveness

I was browsing in a nearby Christian bookstore, when I noticed a sign stating that the owner performed "Resting in the Spirit" services. I had recently read about resting or slaying in the spirit and was curious. As I understood it, the person performing the service places his or her hands on the recipient who would often seem to go to sleep or faint while totally relaxed. I made an appointment for a few days later to meet with the owner to enjoy a restful experience.

When I arrived for my appointment, the owner escorted me to a room in the back of the bookstore. Other than greeting each other, the two of us never spoke to each other. There were two chairs approximately six feet apart facing each other. We took our seats. I was surprised that he wasn't standing and putting his hands on my head or shoulders. I closed my eyes as he began reading a very vivid account of the passion of Christ. I wasn't feeling peaceful at all; instead I suddenly started weeping, knowing that I was a cause of Jesus' suffering and death. My sins had torn his flesh with the spikes of the whip, pushed the thorns into his skull, crushed him under the weight of the cross, pounded the nails into his hands and feet, and thrust the lance into his heart.

The owner kept reading and I kept weeping. When he finished, I noticed that my shirt and pants were drenched. I got up and left the store, embarrassed for having soaked myself. I did have an incredible feeling of peace as I walked away, not the kind I had expected, however. I had received the great gift of grace to feel deep sorrow for my sins.

What kind of a God is this? He not only forgives my sins, he even became a man to suffer and die for me so that I wouldn't pay the price for my sins. Look at what I've done to him through my fault, through my fault, through my most grievous fault, and look at what he's done for me! This is a God I want to know, to follow, and to love with all my heart. I want to avoid sinning because it hurts God who loves me unconditionally. Unfortunately, this experience didn't mean I would never sin again. God still loves me despite my sinfulness. I now understand that I am totally dependent on God's mercy.

If God can forgive my offenses against him, how can I not forgive those who have hurt me? I have known people who are proud of never forgiving someone who has hurt them. They seem to wear their unwillingness to forgive as a badge of honor, as a way of getting even. In fact, it is more like an anchor weighing them down, preventing them from being lifted up by the peace that comes from forgiveness. Several years ago I was blessed to receive the grace to forgive in the following situation, which provided a valuable lesson on sharing God's love with others.

There was an individual, I will call George, who had caused me a great deal of harm. Unfortunately, I wasn't in a position to stop him. I tried to avoid him as much as possible. A couple of months after my conversion, George asked me unexpectedly to do him a favor. He was scheduled for heart surgery and needed someone to cover for him at an event taking place on the same day.

My first inclination was to say no, hell no! But before I responded, I asked God for guidance. After praying, I sent George a note agreeing to help, and I told him that in this difficult time I could give him only two things—my friendship and my prayers—and that he had them both. Where did my response come from?

I subsequently felt a strong desire to pray for George daily. I prayed that God would bless him and fill him with the grace to desire a conversion of heart, if needed. I haven't seen George for several years. I still pray for him daily, and I often wonder where George is and how he's doing. He has never acknowledged the note. It doesn't matter. I thought that maybe someday when I'm in heaven, I will feel someone tapping me on the shoulder, and it will be George. As I turn around, he'll say to me "Thanks, Al, for praying for me. I finally saw the light and it changed my life. Let's share the joy in heaven together."

I like to believe that *to forgive is to receive.* What did I receive by forgiving George? I received peace and the grace to see him as a child of God. I received the joy of praying for his well-being and hoping that I was helping him in his journey to heaven. Maybe the joy I receive in heaven will be magnified by sharing in George's heavenly joy. Isn't that what it's all about?

| 7 |

A Needed Course Correction

It would be nice if I only had to surrender to God once in my life, or if the process of transformation would move quickly on a smooth, uninterrupted path. Unfortunately, neither is the case. I must constantly examine my life to recognize when I have failed to surrender to God's will, when I need a course correction to guide me back to Room 104, and then on to room 105. Transformation takes a lifetime and doesn't necessarily follow a straight line.

In the months following my conversion I had felt much closer to God and had experienced the joy of forgiveness. But did my actions reflect what I was learning? I soon learned a painful lesson: I had not made much progress at all.

My daughter and I went to the grocery store one

evening. As we headed to the express checkout lane, I noticed an elderly man with a scowl on his face, slowly shuffling his feet while pushing his cart towards the same lane. I instantly calculated the speed and the angle that I needed to traverse in order to cut him off. My calculations were accurate as I slipped in line a few feet in front of him. As I triumphantly pushed the cart out of the store, my daughter told me that I hadn't been very nice to cut in front of the elderly man. At first, I was surprised that she had corrected me, but then I realized she was right. What was I thinking, or not thinking? Was the ice re-forming in Mr. Blockhead?

Later that evening I went to pray in my parish chapel. The chapel was empty as I knelt down, closed my eyes and relaxed. After a few minutes, I sensed an inner voice saying "Allan, you have a problem with the sick and elderly. Take off early from work tomorrow and volunteer at a local nursing home."

I left work early the next day and drove to the nursing home. The nun in charge directed me to the head of activities. After a short discussion, we agreed that I could visit two of the male residents who had no regular visitors. This was a unique experience for me. No one had asked me to do this; no one required me to do it; I was doing this on my own, although with some prompting from an inner voice. I had not volunteered to do anything like this before.

I agreed to visit Fred and Joe for an hour each on Saturday afternoons when my schedule allowed. Over time we became good friends. I felt privileged that they had welcomed me into their lives and shared their stories and family pictures with me. The experience was remarkable; it was a mutual sharing of affection between men without any expectations or requirements.

Following this experience, I eagerly sought other volunteer opportunities. I used to skim over requests for volunteers in my parish bulletin; now I often responded quickly so that I didn't miss a chance to serve. Jesus has asked me to love with his heart and I had learned how that feels. I now understood that this was the abundant life promised by Jesus. By sharing the Divine life of God's love, the Divine life in me is increased in return. This was a much needed course correction.

8

May I Have This Dance?

I had just spent a three-day weekend on my first silent retreat. It was the first time I had been able to spend so many hours alone in prayer and reflection without the normal distractions of daily life—no phones, no laptops or other devices, no newspapers, no television. The quiet of the retreat provided a unique opportunity to hear God speaking in the silence of my heart.

The afternoon after returning home from the retreat, I leaned back in my recliner and listened to beautiful instrumental music. What happened next was immediate and totally unexpected. I was standing on a sandy beach with the waves from a large body of water on my right lapping the shore at my feet. In the distance I could see a man walking toward me. As he got closer, I felt that it was Jesus. I took His outstretched hands and we began to dance. As we swirled around, I couldn't stop looking into his eyes. They were unlike any eyes I had ever seen. They radiated an overwhelming sense of peace and joy. It is hard to describe how both feelings simultaneously permeated my body. I was completely relaxed, yet it felt as though every cell in my body was dancing.

We danced for a couple of minutes. We swirled each other around, then let go of each other's hands, dancing in a circle as we raised our arms skyward. The music slowly ended. The last thing I remember was looking into his eyes, seeing the love in his smile and feeling the most overwhelming sense of peace. I then opened my eyes.

Whether this was merely a dream, or whether it took place somewhere between sleep and consciousness, I don't know. Perhaps it was a vision seen through the eyes of my heart. It seemed as though I was awake; it felt so real. I will never forget it, no matter what it was.

A few weeks later I asked the pastor at our church to help me understand the experience. He suggested that I not analyze it but just accept it as a gift. It truly was a gift, one of the most beautiful gifts I've ever received. However, the lawyer in me couldn't resist doing some analysis. I concluded that the dance confirmed three truths: Jesus is alive; he is peace; and he is joy. I guess there's also a fourth truth: he doesn't care if you're a lousy dancer.

Now Jesus asks that I bring others into the dance. This dance is performed by reaching out and serving others, connecting with them in their need. It feels like we are dancing to the heavenly music that continuously fills the universe like cosmic radiation permeating all space. Only after my conversion, when grace opened my ears, could I hear the melody. Since racing the elderly gentleman to the checkout line in the store, I have been blessed to join with Jesus in dancing with many sick and elderly men and women. I have been privileged to serve as a volunteer in a hospital pastoral care department, as an ombudsman at a nursing home, and as a hospice volunteer. I pray that my dance card will never be full.

Who would I be if I hadn't said yes to God's call? How much less of a man would I be? I offered part of myself to each of those I have served, and they in turn have given back to me part of themselves. Since the dance with Jesus, he has given me many opportunities to help people in ways that I would have never previously considered. I picture all of us holding hands, dancing in an ever-expanding circle. As the circle enlarges, I feel myself growing into the person God desires me to be. This is the true meaning of the dance.

When Jesus asks me to dance, I pray that I will always respond, "Yes, Lord, you lead—I'll follow."

9

Keep on Dancing

Sometimes the dance partner Jesus selects isn't one that I would pick. I have learned that even if my partner occasionally steps on my toes, or when the dance seems interminable, I shouldn't stop dancing as long as Jesus is still leading.

For several years I served as a volunteer ombudsman at a local nursing home. My job as a volunteer was basically twofold: (1) to educate residents as to their legal rights as residents of a long-term care facility, and (2) to serve as their advocate with management to resolve any complaints they might have concerning their care. This was purely a secular position and had no religious affiliation.

Before I started my assignment at the nursing home, I met with the administrator to review the home's policies and other details related to my assignment.

The administrator warned me to be aware of Mack (not his real name), who was a particularly difficult resident. Mack had no consideration for others; he watched television with the volume turned up very high all day and night. He was verbally abusive to several members of the nursing home staff, and he often refused care when he didn't like the staff member or disagreed with the way he or she performed a particular task. He was so offensive to every potential roommate that no one lasted more than one day. The administrator's warnings were not only accurate, they turned out to be grossly understated.

I visited Mack almost every week for the next three years. My primary purpose was to help him get the special care he needed. Unfortunately, Mack's negative attitude often worked to his detriment, as staff members would leave his room immediately after Mack had insulted them, even if they weren't finished with his care. Often staff wouldn't enter his room in order to avoid a confrontation.

Mack detested the other residents and only left his room to go to a doctor's appointment. He told me on several occasions that I didn't need to continue to visit him. Despite his negative attitude, I continued to visit Mack on a regular basis. His social worker told me that he had no immediate family or any visitors.

During one visit Mack told me how he always cursed staff members who said, "God bless you" or mentioned Jesus or God. Mack would shout out an obscenity and order them to leave his room. He told me that he didn't want to talk about God. He was tired of people telling him to be good and threatening hellfire if he didn't change his ways. I decided not to bring up the subject of God unless and until I felt it appropriate.

The opportunity presented itself one day when Mack unexpectedly asked me how much I was paid for my weekly visits to the nursing home. I was surprised that he didn't know that I was a volunteer and received no compensation. He told me that I must be a do-gooder, and, like all do-gooders, I volunteered in order to make myself feel good. I responded that I did feel good about coming, but that was not my motivation.

I told him that my God is a loving God, merciful and forgiving. Despite all the wrongs I had committed, God still loves me and forgives me when I confess my sins and ask for his forgiveness. It was the love of God inside me that called me to share his love with others. I told Mack that I would be glad to talk more about God anytime he wished. He didn't throw me out of the room; he remained silent. I left shortly thereafter.

Over the following several months, Mack and I shared stories about growing up. We both talked about several things we regretted, starting with our teenage years. Once I got past his nasty façade, I discovered that Mack was very intelligent and possessed a good sense of humor. As much as he tried to hide it, he also could be sensitive and caring. When his favorite nurse announced that she was leaving and taking a position with a hospital, Mack thanked her by sending her a dozen red roses in appreciation for her kind and loyal treatment.

During my visits with Mack I would occasionally mention how much happier I am since turning my life over to God and following Jesus. During one visit I felt prompted to ask Mack if he had ever been baptized. He said no, since his parents didn't believe in baptism or going to church. I told him that I could arrange for a minister or priest to meet with him or baptize him if he changed his mind. He declined. I told Mack to let me know if he ever wanted me to baptize him. In order to make sure that I was prepared if Mack ever asked, I consulted with the senior assistant pastor of my parish.

It was almost three years after I started seeing Mack that he moved to another nursing home approximately 30 miles away. At the time of the relocation Mack became seriously ill and spent the next few months moving back and forth between the new nursing home and the hospital. Even though I was no longer acting as his ombudsman, I continued to visit him every couple of weeks as a friend. No family members or friends visited Mack in the nursing home or hospital. I was it.

One day in early December when I entered his room in the nursing home Mack said, "Morning, Al, pour the water on me." He had a large pitcher of water on the tray next to his bed. I told him that even if he was hot, I wouldn't pour water on him. Mack smiled and said, "You don't understand, I want you to baptize me." I was elated. I got a small paper cup from the nurse's station, filled it with water, and baptized him. Wow! I had prayed a long time for this to happen.

For Christmas that year I brought Mack a statue of Jesus. It was the Divine Mercy statue, with rays of red and white streaming from his chest, depicting the blood and water that gushed forth from Jesus' heart after being pierced by a soldier's lance following Jesus' death on the cross. Mack and I discussed the necessity of asking God to forgive our sins in order to avail ourselves of his Divine Mercy.

Mack asked me to put the statue on the table directly across from his bed so he could see it clearly. I visited Mack a few more times at the hospital before he passed away at the end of January.

Neither the hospital nor the nursing home had any record of a relative who could claim Mack's body. The hospital contacted me and asked if I knew anything about Mack's burial wishes. Mack had told me that he wanted to be cremated. The next day I was contacted by the cremation company that had picked up Mack's body. They told me that if no one claimed his ashes, they would be sent to a facility approximately 50 miles away to be labeled and stored with other unclaimed ashes.

I remembered that Mack mentioned that he had served in the United States Army. I mentioned this to the cremation company, and they offered to investigate the possibility of having a military funeral for Mack. They successfully arranged a full military funeral. The honor guard, my wife, my parish priest, and I were the only ones in attendance at the funeral service on that cold February morning.

I remember smiling with a lump in my throat as a recording of "Amazing Grace" played on. After two soldiers in dress uniforms ceremoniously folded Mack's burial flag, they solemnly presented it to me. I thought, "Who am I to receive this flag?" The service concluded with the playing of taps and Monsignor reading prayers for a Christian burial.

It was a crisp fall day several years later when I visited Mack's gravesite. I was glad to see the Christian cross engraved at the top of his headstone. I had been blessed to join Mack on his spiritual journey. He was now at rest.

The warmth of my smile tempered the morning chill, as I reflected on how Mack and I had received such a great outpouring of grace during the brief time we shared. It was grace that emboldened me to talk to Mack about God and encouraged me to persevere. It was grace that led Mack to desire baptism and grace that invited me to be a part of that holy event.

It is grace that gives me hope that someday I will join Mack in heaven "bright shining as the sun."

Oh, what a dance that will be!

PART IV

THE FULLNESS
OF LIFE

WHO AM I, LORD, THAT YOU ASK FOR MY ALL?

Amen, amen, I say to you, unless a grain of wheat falls to the ground and dies, it remains just a grain of wheat; but if it dies, it produces much fruit. Whoever loves his life, loses it, and whoever hates his life in this world will preserve it for eternal life. Whoever serves me must follow me, and where I am, there also will my servant be. The Father will honor whoever serves me.

(John 12: 24-26)

10

Jesus, Teacher of the New Math

Several years ago I took a class related to the Church's teaching on social justice. For my final grade, I made a presentation contending that it is grace that motivates and sustains us in our call to do justice and serve others. Since several of my classmates were elementary teachers seeking a Certificate in Religious Studies, I thought that the title, "Jesus, Teacher of the New Math," might be appealing

Since I have no formal training in theology, I do not feel qualified to give a theology lesson. However, since I enjoyed solving equations in algebra class, I feel qualified to give the following math lesson instead.

To illustrate the nature of a complete human being, I propose the following equation:

$$p^2 = \left\{ \frac{4\pi^2}{[G(m_1 + m_2)]} \right\} R^3 = kR^3$$

The above is not really my equation for a complete human being; I borrowed it from an astronomy book. Don't worry, I won't attempt to use it to calculate the distance man travels away from the Son of God during man's orbital period on earth. I included this equation to illustrate how we can sometimes make matters more complicated than necessary. Accordingly, my equation for a complete human being is as follows:

$$H=h+D$$

Pretty simple. The "H" represents a complete human being. The "h" represents the human component of our nature, comprised of body, soul, and spirit. The "D" represents the Divine component of God's life of grace. A complete human being is the sum of h plus D.

Christianity teaches that as a result of man's original fall from grace (the story of Adam and Eve), the special relationship between God and humanity was broken. Jesus Christ, the Son of God, became man in order to save us from our sins and to restore that relationship. Jesus gave us the sacrament of Baptism through which he transforms our nature. DNA is no longer just an abbreviation for deoxyribonucleic acid. By the infusion of Divine life though the Holy Spirit, we have been elevated to a new DNA: **D**ivine **N**ature by **A**doption.

In receiving a share in God's Divine life, we have been adopted into God's family, the Holy Trinity. We are now brothers and sisters in Christ. As children of God, we are able to fully participate in the greatest power in the universe: God's love. This power can not only transform our lives, it can also transform the entire world.

If we fail to fully embrace the "D" component of our nature, as enhanced by the gift of sanctifying grace that we are blessed to receive throughout our lives, we are limited to a fraction of our potential, and consequently, we fail to enjoy life to its fullest. In such a case, even though we may experience a certain level of success and happiness from time to time, we cheat ourselves out of living an infinitely more rewarding life, filled with the eternal peace and joy of Christ.

Consider two popular slogans recently used to motivate people. One is used for recruiting by the United States Army, "Be all you can be!" How many recruits would sign up if the slogan were changed to "Be only a fraction of all you can be?" Another popular slogan is "Be the best version of yourself." How many people would be motivated to strive for excellence if the phrase were changed to "Be only a fraction of the best version of yourself?"

Jesus is the way, the truth, and the life. He shows us the *way* to live "all that we can be," to be the "best version of ourself." He is the *truth* that leads to the fullness of *life*. Jesus teaches us that in order to participate in the fullness of the life that he promises, we are to love God with all our heart, soul, and mind and to love our neighbor as ourself. These two great commandments are interconnected. Jesus admonishes us that to love God so completely we must keep his commandments and that to love each other so ardently we must also be willing to serve others in their need. Jesus summons us to follow these precepts, not in a passive way, but as a passionate, dynamic response to God's unconditional love for us.

With one life to live, why would we choose not to live it to the fullest? We may not have heard or fully understood the Good News of the Gospel. We may fear the unknown of living differently than we are accustomed. We may be comfortable with the ways things are and not realize how much better our lives could be. We may be mired in our self-centeredness, preferring the power of being in control, making our own rules, saying "No" to God.

We are called to share in the Divine life of God's grace dwelling in us, making us co-heirs to the heavenly kingdom. To maximize the Divine life, we must say "Yes" to God's will. Being the King, God has the legitimate authority to make the rules for his kingdom. Surrendering to God is like taking a loyalty oath to the King, acknowledging his preeminence and submitting to his will.

If we refuse and follow our own rules, we honor ourselves as kings and the makers of our own laws. Since we are then acting as the supreme self, we change the rules whenever we desire. We can also decide there are no rules or apply a different set of rules to others as we wish. Exercising our free will in this way constitutes a rebellion against the rightful King, a rejection of our true nature, and risks the loss of our inheritance. When that happens, we need to approach the throne of the Divine Majesty with humility, confess our transgressions, and ask for God's mercy and forgiveness. By doing so, we will once again be free and experience the incredible joy that emanates from sharing in the Divine life.

St. Ignatius of Loyola, in the First Principle and Foundation of the Spiritual Exercises, states that our ultimate goal is to choose what better leads to God's deepening life in us. Increasing the life-giving grace of the Divine integrates the human component with the Divine component, thereby transforming us into the complete person God desires us to be.

Jesus shared in our humanity, so that we might share in his divinity. As we increase our sharing of the Divine life, C. S. Lewis in *Mere Christianity* says that we are to become "Little Christs." Perhaps C. S. Lewis would simplify my equation for human wholeness to H=H. That is, a complete human being (H) must grow to be holy as God is holy (H), so as to become Christ to the world.

---- 11 ----

I'm All In

My wife, Cyndi, and I were asked several years ago to serve as facilitators in a program preparing couples who were, as the result of divorce or widowhood, getting remarried in the Catholic Church. After a few years of helping couples over a six-week period, we were asked to be speakers on the weekend program for those couples who needed a condensed version of the program.

One of the topics I presented was on commitment. In preparing my presentation I reflected on the two most important relationships in my life: my relationship with my wife and my relationship with my God. Am I fully committed to both relationships? When I was younger, I was motivated to excel in academics (except for the first two years of college when my head was somewhere else) and in sports. I enjoyed the immediate feedback from getting good grades and succeeding in athletic competition. I now realize that I wasn't as fully committed in my marriage or in my relationship with God. Maybe it was because the feedback wasn't immediate, or I wasn't aware of any feedback at all. Making a commitment requires a firm decision to act independently of any expectation of receiving any immediate feedback.

At the altar did I take Cyndi for richer or for poorer, in sickness and in health, and then add, "And I give you my mediocrity?" In other words, how committed am I to our relationship? I need to rise above mediocrity and remind myself on a regular basis that my commitment to love my wife is an unconditional promise.

When I meet Jesus face to face, how will I account for my life? If Jesus says, "Allan, I suffered and died for you. How did you respond to my great love for you?" I hope I don't look down and answer shamefully, "Lord, I gave you my mediocrity." Before my conversion, I was mostly lukewarm in my belief that Jesus is the Son of God and indifferent to what effect that should have in my life. It was like I was sitting on a fence unwilling to seriously consider who Jesus was, what he taught, or whether I should make any effort to get to know, love, and follow him. That approach got me nowhere. The only thing I got from sitting on the fence was splinters in my bum.

God desires and deserves a complete commitment from us, not mediocrity. We need to strive to subordinate our wills completely to his. God has given us everything. When we respond appropriately, we experience his freedom and a degree of peace and joy in this life that is a foretaste of the unimaginable peace and joy we will experience in heaven for eternity.

Imagine that I'm sitting at a poker table. There are several stacks of poker chips in front of me. Each chip is a different color, representing every unique facet of my being. The dealer asks if I want to call the final bet, which will take all of my chips, or fold my hand. I push all my chips into the middle of the table, and announce to the dealer, "I'm all in." I'm confident that I have a winning hand. It's like that with Jesus. I want to trust him completely, to bet my life on him, to make a total commitment to know, love, and follow him with my whole heart. When I meet him after this life, I hope I can say, "My Lord and Savior, you have been my brother and my best friend. Thank you for all you have given me. I did my best to give you my all."

I wrote the following prayer to keep my focus on the primacy of God in my life. I say the prayer each morning and several times each day. It helps me to keep God at the center of my life and offer him my love, praise, and thanksgiving. It also reminds me to

seek his grace to help me serve him through others
and fulfill the purpose for which he created me.

HEAVENLY FATHER

I love you for who you are.
I praise you and give you thanks for the gift of
your Son, for your mercy and forgiveness, for
my family, my friends and all that I have.

I give you this day and ask for your grace that
I may serve you with faith, hope and love in
all that I do, and that I may be the person you
desire me to be.

Amen

CONCLUSION

I present these final comments in the form of an imaginary account at the closing of a trial.

JUDGE: Mr. Barton, I have been asked to render a decision on your true identity and the proximate cause of your alleged transformation from the person you were before October 1989 (a.k.a., the "Old Al") into the person you now claim to be (a.k.a., the "New Al"). Before I enter a judgment, I have a few comments on the evidence before this court.

First, I find the facts stated in your book, which was admitted into evidence as Exhibit A, to be credible, although some of your reflections are somewhat unusual.

Second, I note that most of the witnesses who testified about the actions of the Old Al did so reluctantly, only after being subpoenaed. Perhaps their hesitation was caused by their warm affection for you, or by their own complicity in some of the events that took place before your alleged conversion. In the interest of all concerned, I will grant the motion to place the testimony related to the Old Al under seal.

Third, your book describes events demonstrating several very significant changes in the thoughts and actions of the New Al compared to the Old Al. I note that no witness has contradicted your account of such a miraculous transformation.

Fourth, I find that most of the physical evidence submitted is inconclusive. Exhibit B (a picture of the Old Al) and Exhibit C (a picture of the New Al) are very similar. Let the record show that the new Al does look very much like the Old Al, with certain changes, which are to be expected of one a lot older. The New Al has larger ears and nose, a receding hairline, and much whiter hair. I will also note that there are a couple of significant differences between the two pictures. There is a radiant gleam in the eyes of the New Al, and his smile is much softer.

Furthermore, Exhibits D and E containing the medical records of the Old Al and the New Al, respectively, are also of questionable evidentiary value. Most of the differences are explained simply by the advancement of age. There is one significant change, however, for which no medical explanation has been offered. The chest x-ray of the New Al shows a heart larger than the one of the Old Al. The doctor's notes indicate that the enlarged heart has not resulted from congestive heart failure or other physical cause. Therefore, Mr. Barton, at your request, I will take judicial notice of the spiritual phenomenon that Dr. Theodor Seuss Geisel discovered that had caused the Grinch's heart to grow larger. That miracle occurred one Christmas morning in Whoville as the Grinch discovered the joy of self-giving love.

JUDGE: Mr. Barton, as I was never a math whiz, do you offer any mathematical proof of your equation for a complete human being that is contained in Chapter 10 of your book?

MR. BARTON: Thank you, Your Honor. My proof is not based on any mathematical certainty, but on my deductions from a lifetime of experiences. Jesus promised us an abundant life, a life where we are able to reach our full potential as human beings created in God's image and likeness. To do this, God desires that we use all the gifts of our human nature in harmony with the divine nature God shares with us. I know that when I surrender to God's will and act in accordance with God's plan for the integration of both components, I feel the joy of a man fully alive, more complete, more solid, more real. When I fail to live as God desires, I feel like I am only a shadow of myself with no substance.

I feel real when I smile at a passing stranger, or when I say a kind word to the checker at the grocery store, or the wait staff at a restaurant, particularly when I sense they're having a difficult time. I am filled with joy when I look into the eyes of certain hospital patients to whom I have just given Holy Communion and sense that the Jesus in them is looking at the Jesus in me and smiling. I feel satisfaction when I see the smiles of the nursing home residents after helping them solve a problem with their care. I feel fully alive when I hold the hand of a hospice patient in the final hours before death.

JUDGE: Thank you, Mr. Barton. I have decided to ask your readers for their input before I render a decision on the issues before this court. Before I do so, do you have any final words for your readers?

MR. BARTON: Thank you, Your Honor. To my readers: First, I would like to thank you for your patience in reaching the conclusion of these proceedings. Second, I pray that you will give your "Yes" to God, ask him to show you who you really are, and ardently pursue your God-given purpose in life. For those who do, God has promised that you will receive the fullness of life with the incredible peace and joy that follow. I can't imagine how wonderful the joy will be at the heavenly banquet, if the joy we experience in this life is only an appetizer.

Finally, I pray that I will one day be able to serve you at the heavenly banquet, and I hope to join you in the dance that follows.

APPENDIX

Behold the Heart of Jesus

While attending a silent retreat several years ago, I had a very unusual experience that inspired me to write the poem below. I was walking back to my room one night after the last presentation in the chapel when I stopped and gazed at the full orange moon suspended in the sky above the Mississippi River. When I looked at the moon more closely, I visualized a beating human heart.

I am not a poet; I hadn't written a poem since third grade. I didn't intend to write this poem, but when I returned to my room, I picked up my legal pad and began to write. I finished the poem the next day after observing a dazzling sunrise.

As a lawyer for 40 years, I always wrote with a specific purpose in mind, carefully crafting documents intended to accomplish a particular purpose. Writing this poem was an entirely different experience; it poured freely from my heart with little conscious effort and no preconceived objective.

For many years the poem has reminded me in a very vivid way of Jesus' invitation to share intimately in the love and Divine Mercy that emanate from the depths of his Sacred Heart. Jesus is the Way, leading us through the darkness of our lives with his resplendent light. He is the Truth, leading us in the daylight of our lives with the blazing fire of his Eternal Word. He is the Life, leading us to completeness with the fervent embrace of his Eternal Love.

The poem I wrote in third grade was about a flying zebra. I believe that I will always remember the words of that poem and of the Behold the Heart of Jesus poem, since I must have written them on my heart with indelible ink. I don't know if I will write another poem, but if I do, I hope I will continue to look upwards for my inspiration.

BEHOLD THE HEART OF JESUS

The orange moon rises above the cold river,
stirring my soul and stroking me gently in the
bosom of God's love.
It is a fitting color for my mood tonight,
hanging somewhere between the crimson flame
of passion and the pale yellow of serenity.
Behold the Heart of Jesus, burning with the fire of
divine love and beating to the pulse of His eternal peace.

A lover's blush warms the icy night air
with memories of her groom's soft touch.
A ragged beggar unfolds his craggy palms,
splintered by the wooden hearts of a thousand passers-by.
The darkness shrouds the dreams and despairs
of all mankind, loved into being to know the fullness of life.

Rising above the cloud of unknowing,
the sun radiates the light of truth.
Behold the Heart of Jesus, lifting the
veil of ignorance and illuminating the minds
and hearts of all God's children.

ACKNOWLEDGMENTS

I wish to give special thanks to the following individuals who helped me complete this book. The words on these pages have been bouncing around in my head for several years, and would never have settled down long enough to land in a book without your help.

To the Holy Spirit for keeping the vivid memories alive in my head and heart, and for the wakeup calls at 4:00 a.m. for our writing sessions.

To Monsignor Timothy Cronin for your encouragement.

To my wife, Cyndi, for your support and encouragement, especially for acting as my sounding board (without appearing to be bored).

To Cathy Gilmore for your encouragement and creative input, especially for helping select the title.

To Trese Gloriod for your spectacular cover design and book layout.

To Katie Hall for your gracious words of encouragement.

To Zip Rzeppa for your advice, support and encouragement. You have been my manager, coach, teammate, and cheerleader, all in one. Without your help, I would never had gotten up to the plate.

ABOUT THE AUTHOR

Allan "Al" Barton, retired attorney, lives with his wife, Cyndi, in St. Louis County, Missouri.